MW00475531

Follow us on Facebook+Twitter @GMNOTEBOOK

73538487R00074

Made in the USA
Lexington, KY
09 December 2017